Understanding
Of Detectives a

William Coscarelli, Professor Emeritus
Curriculum and Instruction
Southern Illinois University at Carbondale, 62901-4610
E-mail: coscarel@siu.edu

I hope this helps, in some small way, successful thinking -- for my retirement funds! thanks, Bill

This is an introduction to the *Decision-Making Style Inventory*. For more information about the inventory and it's workshop please search Decision-Making Style Inventory at www.wiley.com or visit
http://decisonmakingstyleinventory.blogspot.com/

Copyright © 2009 by William C. Coscarelli. All rights reserved—though I have no reservations about Teri's systematic style in the editing process

No part of this publication may be reproduced or transmitted in any form or by any means, electronic or mechanical, including photocopy, recording, or any information storage and retrieval system, without the express written permission of the author.

CONTENTS

UNDERSTANDING UN-UNDERSTANDABLE PEOPLE 1

ASSESSING YOUR OWN STYLE [PART 1] 4

THE PRIMARY COLORS OF THE DMSI 10

STRUCTURAL STYLE: SPONTANEOUS & SYSTEMATIC 22

TREASURE HUNTERS AND DETECTIVES 33

PROCESSING STYLE: EXTERNAL & INTERNAL 44

THE FOUR BLENDED STYLES OF THE *DMSI* 47

SUMMARY OF THE DMSI THEORY 49

ASSESSING YOUR OWN STYLE [PART 2] 53

THE STYLES IN ACTION 54

ADAPTING YOUR STYLE 66

WHY THESE FOUR STYLES? 67

REFERENCES 70

UNDERSTANDING UN-UNDERSTANDABLE PEOPLE

Let me begin with two examples of styles in action:

> "Neil Armstrong was typical of the new breed. A lot of people couldn't figure out Armstrong...His expression hardly ever changed. You'd ask him a question, and he would just stare at you with those pale-blue eyes of his, and you'd start to ask the question again, figuring he hadn't understood, and--click-- out of his mouth would come forth a sequence of long quiet, perfectly formed, precisely thought-out sentences..."
>
> --Tom Wolfe, *The Right Stuff*, p. 416

> "When Gary Davis (campaign manager for then California governor, now Oakland, CA mayor, Jerry Brown) asked if he (Brown) wanted to issue a statement of objectives:
>
> > 'What do you mean?' inquired Brown.
> > 'Well,' said Davis, 'What are you trying to do?'
> > 'It'll emerge.' said Brown...
>
> His conferences are movable feasts of words, with no agenda and frequent changes of venue...'I like to think out loud'...'I write my speeches when I take that last drink of water before I get up to speak.'"
>
> --*Newsweek*, April 23, 1997, p. 27

These two men represent very different styles in decision-making. Each would find the other difficult to work with if they didn't know how to identify and adjust to these styles.

The *Decision-Making Style Inventory* describes two dimensions in decision-making styles, which I have classified as structural and processing dimensions:

- A person's structural style--how they seek, organize, and weigh information--can be either Systematic or Spontaneous. The Systematic prefers logical processes and the analysis of parts in a problem. The Spontaneous prefers thought chaining and tends to focus on the whole, not the parts.

- The processing style--how people will make sense of the information in their structural style--can be Internal or External. The Internal prefers to analyze privately. The External *needs* to hear the words to analyze information.

- The two dimensions, like primary colors, are combined to find one of four preferred styles: Systematic-Internal, Systematic-External, Spontaneous-Internal, and Spontaneous-Eternal.

Thus, Neil Armstrong--the Systematic Internal--would find working with Jerry Brown--the Spontaneous External--difficult. However, by understanding the differences in these styles and learning to draw on different styles for different situations, people can become better decision makers as well as better friends, partners, and colleagues.

Statistically speaking, the *DMSI* styles don't overlap much with other styles such as the Myers-Briggs. There is no implication of "right" or "wrong," "smart" or "dumb." People differ in many ways and have found that the *DMSI* theory is an easily understandable way to understand un-understandable people.

ASSESSING YOUR OWN STYLE [PART 1]

Here is a chance to begin to think about your own style before we explore the theory in more detail.

    1. On the next page read each description at the ends of the bold line and make a mark where you think you would be on that vertical line.

I move from goal to goal in a deliberate manner. I am very aware of setting goals or tasks and don't like to deviate from the goal until it is accomplished. I approach decisions in an analytical way. Having made a choice I will evaluate it by examining the consequences of the choice. I tend to be more tempered in an assessment of an event — avoiding extreme reactions.

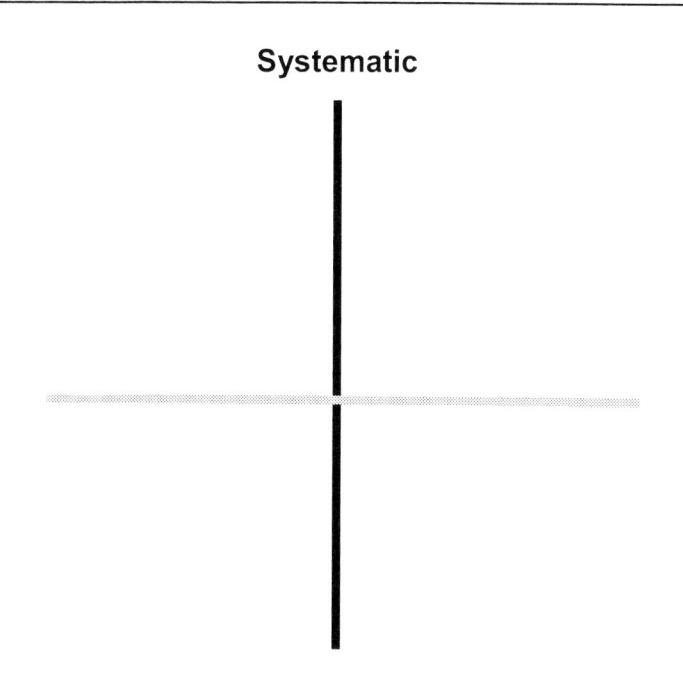

Systematic

Spontaneous

I move from goal to goal easily and without deliberate thought. I change goals easily. My thought processes tend to be chaining. I prefer to act on an idea rather than think about it. I tend to evaluate my actions as something to like or dislike in a global "big picture" way.

2. On the next page read each description at the ends of the bold line and make a mark where you think you would be on that horizontal line.

I prefer to organize my thoughts privately before speaking.

If pressed to discuss an issue I haven't thought about — and especially if it is an important decision — I can become irritated.

Internal ═══════════════ **External**

I need to think out loud. I won't be certain of a decision unless I have the opportunity to talk about it.

I prefer, even need, to hear my own words in order to make

3. Now plot the intersection of these two points. You will end up in one our four quadrants. Here is an example:

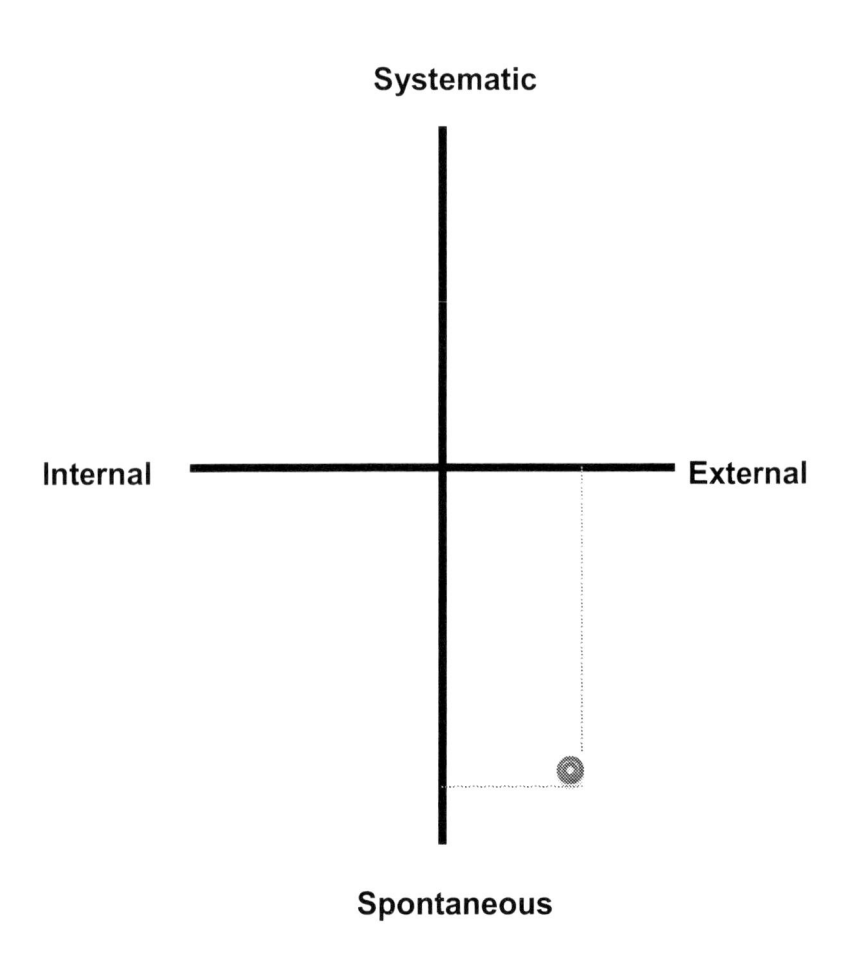

Systematic

Internal ──────────┼────────── **External**

Spontaneous

4. Here are the quadrants that represent the four styles the *DMSI* assesses. Circle the quadrant that represents your style. Keep in mind you've just taken an informal style assessment—the *DMSI* will be much more accurate—but as you read more you can compare your assessment with the more detailed descriptions and refine your self assessment.

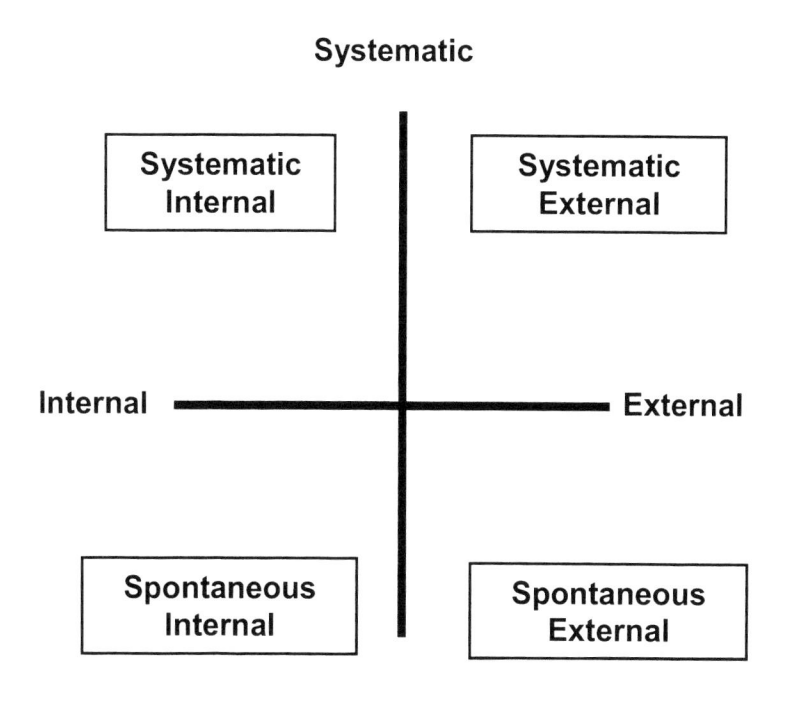

Systematic

| Systematic Internal | Systematic External |

Internal ──────────┼────────── **External**

| Spontaneous Internal | Spontaneous External |

Spontaneous

THE PRIMARY COLORS OF THE DMSI

The *DMSI* theory shows us two information gathering styles (Systematic and Spontaneous) and two processing styles (Internal and External). These are primary colors, so to speak; and like the blending of shades on a color wheel, each of us blends a gathering style and a processing style to form four new styles:

- Systematic-Internal
- Systematic –External
- Spontaneous-Internal
- Spontaneous-External

To get a sense of these decision-making lifestyles I want to discuss the primary colors first in this section, and then venture into the blended styles.

Systematic

Systematics have a tendency to seek perfection. Their tendency would be to over-prepare and over-analyze a situation. There is a story of President Warren G. Harding who is quoted as saying to a friend "John, I can't make a damn thing out of this problem. I listen to one side and they seem right, and then God! I talk to the other side and they seem just as right, and there I am where I started…God, what a job!" This is a classic case of analysis paralysis where the Systematic sees so many reasons they can become paralyzed in deciding.

When looking at life, the Systematic will link past, present, and future, perhaps placing a greater emphasis on the role of the past in understanding the present. In general, the Systematic will have difficulty adapting or adopting a Spontaneous style.

[My studies are based on Euro-centric middle-class respondents and about 80% of the samples are Systematic.]

Spontaneous

The Spontaneous is activity driven, not goal driven. They have a tendency to under prepare, and will often have difficulty justifying their choices. They are easily sidetracked during the decision making process and more easily affected by their emotions than the Systematic — they can carry the excitement or sadness of some other aspect of their life into the decision making process and allow emotion to become an important part of their processes. Spontaneouses move with great speed, which often causes them not to see steps in the decision process and hence often can't recount them.

While life is cause-effect for the Systematic, for the Spontaneous the past is disconnected from the present. The present and the future are much more powerful to the Spontaneous than for the Systematic. The Spontaneous can chain not only on ideas and emotions, but on visual cues as well — one image reminding them of another and then another, etc. Wiggle a pencil in front of a Spontaneous and they will stare at *it* — the Systematic will stare at *you* annoyed if you try it with them! One of the more interesting aspects of Spontaneouses is what happens when they lose something. They will look for it in a spontaneous manner —

rarely stopping to systematically think about where they were when they last had it and what they did between then and now. Variety is valued over depth. A Spontaneous would prefer a cocktail party with many interactions to a formal party with one dinner partner seated next to them for the duration of the meal (A Systematic preference, though).

In the chaining process that typifies Spontaneous thought, they often will think they have mentioned an idea to people, but will in fact have never done so. They would describe a situation as one might a picture—with no beginning or end. If they have to deal with systematic problem solving, they'd much prefer problem solving approach such as Synectics. They can engage in Systematic thought, but it will tire them and they will seek to abandon it as soon as feasible. The only way a strong Spontaneous can write and outline for a paper is to write the paper first and then do the outline (I speak from personal knowledge here— such was my high school English experience.) The Spontaneous anthem might be "Things emerged that I hadn't planned on."

This is an example of the classic Spontaneous, from National Public Radio's *Car Talk*:

> **I decide to wash the car; I start toward the garage and notice the mail on the table. OK, I'm going to wash the car, but first I'm going to go through the mail. I lay the car keys down on the desk, discard the junk mail and I notice the trash can is full. OK, I'll just put the bills on my desk and take the trash can out, but since I'm going to be**

near the mailbox anyway, I'll pay these few bills first. Now, where is my check book? OOPS, there's only one check left. My extra checks are in my desk.

Oh, there's the Coke I was drinking. I'm going to look for those checks. But first I need to put my Coke further away from the computer, or maybe I'll pop it into the fridge to keep it cold for a while. I head towards the kitchen and my flowers catch my eye; they need some water. I set the Coke on the counter and ooh, oh! There are my glasses. I was looking for them all morning! I'd better put them away first. I fill the container with water and head for the flower pots —aaaaagh! Someone left the TV remote in the kitchen. We will never think to look in the kitchen tonight when we want to watch television so I'd better put it back in the family room where it belongs. I throw the remote onto a soft cushion on the sofa and I head back down the hall trying to figure out what it was I was going to do.

END OF DAY: The car isn't washed, the bills are unpaid, the Coke is sitting on the kitchen counter, the flowers are half watered, the check book still only has one check in it and I can't seem to find my car keys! When I try to figure out how come nothing got done today, I'm baffled because I KNOW I WAS BUSY ALL DAY LONG!!!

Finally, while Spontaneouses are often viewed as flighty or disorganized in our culture, the problem is apparently not new. Leonardo Di Vinci himself faced a similar problem. In his writings in the Codex Leicester he reflected on his own thinking in Cases and Inventions, almost apologizing:

> **Therefore you will not wonder nor will you laugh at me, Reader, if I make such great leaps from one subject to another.**

[About 20% of my sample is Spontaneous.]

Internal

Internals have a tendency to want to do things all by themselves. They want time to sort out their issues and will become annoyed and inarticulate if asked to justify or make a decision before they have the time for privacy. They may ask others what options seem best for a particular decision, but in the end will make the choice privately. Their introspection can be so powerful to them that they sometimes think they have said something, but in reality have only thought it. I know of an instance in an office where the computers all went down. Everyone in the office was Internal and it was nearly 3 hours before anyone compared notes to find that the whole system wasn't working.

When dealing with an Internal, one can watch for the imperceptible pause when asking for an opinion or such. Especially if they are an Amiable, the Internal won't disagree at first, but will offer an alternative. In some ways, Bob Green captured the essence of an extreme Internal with an interview of former president Richard Nixon (who was also a Systematic).

> "I never wanted to buddy-buddy," he said. "Not only with the press. Even with close friends. I don't believe in letting your hair down, confiding this and that and the other thing-saying, 'Gee, I couldn't sleep because I was worrying...'
>
> "I believe you should keep your troubles to yourself. That's just the way I am. Some people think it's good therapy to sit with a close friend and, you know, just spill your guts. Not me. No way."
>
> Green continued, saying that on the surface such an attitude might promise a person self-protection, but that in the end it would probably result in his being so isolated, and so remote that no one truly knew him.
>
> "Yeah," Nixon said. "It's true. And it's not necessary for them to know."
>
> --*American Beat*, 1983, p.77

One of the more interesting dynamics of the Internal world often shows up in ordering at a new restaurant. This was captured in a conversation from the book *Mysteries of Pittsburgh*.

> "We lifted our menus and complained over the gilt tops about the hot weather. My eyes flitted blindly across the cirrate names of pastas; I

have never been able to read a menu and talk at the same time. I managed to maneuver my father and Phlox into a conversation about the library, and took advantage of these thirty seconds to select ravioli filled with sausage."

--p.173

Likewise, Peter Uberroth who successfully directed a USA Olympic campaign was famous for excusing himself to go to the bathroom—to sit alone in a stall—when he felt he needed to escape from a meeting to organize his thoughts

I always think that Internals go to church and the Externals go to Sunday school.

[About 54% of my sample is Internal.]

External

If our society finds Spontaneous behavior perplexing, Externals are at an even greater disadvantage it seems. Here is Ann Landers capturing a common reaction to Externality, while recognizing at some level the need some have for it:

> **Dear Ann:** After reading in your column about the mother (who) was getting a bit dingy because she talked to herself, I agree with you that talking to oneself is a good way to relieve stress. I have always felt that if you can't talk to yourself, who can you talk to? A few years ago while on vacation in Estes National park my brother walked into the room while I was watching the TV and

caught me talking to myself. He asked, "Mike, are you talking to yourself?" I replied "Yes. Do you mind? It's a private conversation."

Externality is often seen as "dingy" but for many people actually hearing the words is how they know what they think or feel. Prince Charles of England has found the political problems with this style. Many of his associates report that "he has a tendency to think out loud — only to be surprised when the results show up in newspapers." (*Newsweek*, 1979) A former chancellor at Southern Illinois Unversity spoke about this issue several years ago:

> Another thing I do that administrators should not do is think out loud. As a faculty member, you're allowed that luxury to test ideas against other people and to sort of think together as you're discussing things. Well, when you become an administrator, people expect you to speak in conclusions, and if you start thinking aloud people misinterpret what you say as conclusive statements.

On a more cerebral note, though Wilson (1991) wrote about Abraham Lincoln:

> In fact, much to the annoyance of his law partner, Lincoln did his office reading aloud, claiming that both hearing and seeing the words reinforced his grasp of the material.

When one race driver was asked how he prepares for a race (Riggs, 2005) he replied:

> "I talk my way through the section out loud to myself—like my own co-driver. "I'll say. 'Remember the uphill; turn in early; there's a right-hander coming up."

Another sportsman who is a professional croquet player was observed as making "the pauses in the game interesting." (Indianapolis Star, 1982).

> "He has amusing little habits punctuated by hand gestures…He talks to himself, and you can watch him propose and erase strategy in midair."

The need for externality has also been documented with Frank Lloyd Wright (*Newsweek*, 1979):

> More fascinating still is the genesis of Fallingwater, the great 1935 house built for Edger J. Kaufman outside Pittsburgh during Tafel's apprenticeship. First, Wright had paced the 2,000 –acre site with Kaufman. What were his client's favorite vistas, Wright asked? Where did he like to sit? Then Wright began to draw, talking to himself all the while: "Liliane and E.J. will have tea on the balcony. They'll cross the bridge to walk into the woods…The rock on which E.J. sits will be

the hearth, coming right out of the floor, the fire burning behind it. The warming kettle...will swing into the fire, boiling the water. Steam will permeate the atmosphere. You'll hear the hiss." Nothing could illustrate more vividly Wright's sensual approach to what he called "organic architecture."

The writing process is also about externality for many. The process of putting words onto paper (or the screen) is one of externality. E.M. Forester who wrote *Room with View* and *Passage to India*, among other titles, wrote once "How do I know what I think until I see what I say?" The novelist Stephen King talked about his writing in 1997 and observed that the process of putting the words down provided him a way to understand himself: "I write twice because I want to know what I think as well as what I feel."

While our society tends to value the Internal perspective, certain arenas drift toward a preference for Externality. Committee work is usually biased toward those who speak. Television is another area. In *Mediaspeak*, Cross (1983) observes of television shows:

"Most hosts are grateful just to get someone who will fill the room with sound. One talk show booker comments, " We look for the guest who is sure to talk no matter what. Ten seconds of silence appears very awkward on television; thirty seconds is disastrous. A guest who's got to stop to think about everything he says before he opens his mouths is a ratings nightmare." A different booker adds, "Yes, we look for a good looking astronomer who can talk over someone who hesitates before every answer—what he is talking *about* isn't that important."

This kind of attitude rewards glibness and makes hesitancy look like stupidity. As critic Gilbert Seldes says, it puts "a premium on speed…on the quickness rather than the quality of wit and has somehow equated the process of contemplation—the painstaking working out of judgment, the careful consideration of what has been said before replying—with slow-wittedness, with the stooge for the popular comedian's brightness.

"Even as an ex-president," says one talent coordinator, "we wouldn't have used George Washington on our show. Mr. Dullsville in person. He might have been first in the hearts of his countrymen, but today he'd be dragging his bottom in the ratings."

Externals might make good guests, and at the restaurant, they are probably the ones who want to know what everyone else is having to eat; but they do have to work very hard to censor their thoughts. I have two cartoons that capture two competing forces within an External: need for censorship and need for speech.

Moe, the Bully approaches Calvin. "I'm gonna pound you at recess, Twinky. Calvin replies, "You'd better be nice to me, Moe." "Haw! Why? "Because someday my tax dollars will be paying for your prison cell." POW! Calvin learns the first lesson of Externality, "My whole problem is my lips move when I think."

--Calvin & Hobbes, December 9, 1993

In Peanuts, Marcie and Lucy rest against a tree and Marcie asks "Do they have prayer in your school?" "No. But last year they had us observe a "moment of silence." "How did that work?" replies Marcie. "It almost killed me!" observes Lucy.

--Peanuts, November 16, 1985

[About 46% of my sample is External.]

STRUCTURAL STYLE: SPONTANEOUS & SYSTEMATIC

The two types of Structural Styles—Systematic and Spontaneous—vary in five major characteristics of information gathering:

- goal orientation,
- choosing among alternatives,
- thinking patterns,
- risk level,
- and reaction to events.

Goal Orientation

When dealing with Systematics, one is dealing with a person who is very focused and goal-oriented. For instance, a person, who at 16 years old says, 'I want to be a physician' may begin studying the appropriate courses, and everything is then focused to reach that goal. Somewhere along the way that person may decide he doesn't want to be a physician, but he will logically think about it and talk about it.

Systematic individuals move from goal to goal in a deliberate manner; they are aware of setting goals or tasks and moving from one to another. Having established a goal, they are not likely to deviate from the goal until it is accomplished or determined to be inappropriate. When necessary, systematic individuals can be flexible in changing their plans, but they usually must first establish new goals for the new plans. They will typically have a high need to establish long-range goals such as career choice, as well as more immediate ones such as choosing an evening's entertainment.

Here is the type of advice you'd get from a Systematic on buying a car:

> You have decided to buy a new car…. You go home and tell your parents or spouse about your decision, and you are immediately asked "Why do you want (that car)"?
> What will you answer? Will you just say, "because I like (the car?)" If you do, you can be pretty well assured that the response will be something like, "Are you crazy? That's no answer!" From that point on you will be on the losing side of the argument, because you have created little confidence in your decision.
> Imagine, however. That your initial answer had been something like, "I've been late to work so often because of the bus that I'm in danger of losing my job. Second, with the money I've saved in the last year and a half, I can easily afford (the car), which is, you know, an economy car. And oh yes, (it) gets close to thirty miles per gallon of gas." A well thought –out, point-by-point message like that will go a long way toward putting you in the driver's seat.
>
> -Strain & Wysong, *Communication Skills*, p.185

This advice seems to mirror the expected way of deciding in our American culture. I guess this isn't surprising since I find that Systematics are about 80% of the population I have assessed.

    Spontaneous goal orientation is really quite different. I started graduate school in Utah. In the course of driving to the mountains, my used car began to fall apart. We rented an apartment, and since we had no furniture, we went out to buy a sofa. Even though we went to get a sofa, we thought we would also window shop, and so we walked a few blocks to a motorcycle shop.

    I began to think how a motorcycle could be nice in Utah; we started talking about its possible uses. A motorcycle could be driven around the beautiful canyons in Utah. I was pretty weak; it sounded like a good idea. But it wasn't long before my wife suggested, 'Well, sometimes it rains here though', and after all, we were having problems with the car.

    There was this Ford dealership down the road, and we talked to the salesperson there about the cars. 'Yeah, all these Pintos are pretty neat', I thought. And you know, what happened never fazed me. I never really figured it out, and I never really cared. I called my Dad, and told him we had been out to get a new sofa, and we had bought a new car. There was a deep, silent pause that had to work its way across the United States telephone lines from Pennsylvania to Utah.

    Our actions were not goal oriented, and my Dad, the engineer, just thought it was part of my general craziness that he had hoped I would have outgrown. (I haven't really.)

    The spontaneous person will move from goal to goal easily and without deliberate thought. An established goal is easily forgotten or changed. Flexibility in goals is a hallmark of spontaneous individuals. They can establish goals for themselves but will rarely pursue them in the same methodical manner as the systematic individual.

Choosing among alternatives

When it comes to choosing among alternatives, a Systematic wants to analyze what's happening, and to consider the plusses and minuses. To think, 'What are the consequences of doing that?'

When faced with a decision, systematic and spontaneous individuals take radically different approaches to choosing among the alternatives. Spontaneous individuals will personalize the alternatives to evaluate them; they will internally commit to an alternative to determine whether or not they like it. The internal commitment will usually result in excitement about the new ideas, alternative thoughts, persons, and so on.

Spontaneous individuals will change a commitment as quickly as they committed in the first place and may get equally excited about the next alternative. They are not being "wishy-washy." This personalization is their way of determining how they feel about the alternative. They must live with the idea, however briefly, to feel what it would be like. Based on this feeling, they will accept or reject an alternative. They do not always act on every feeling of commitment and may be cautious about actions, but on the whole, they will be seen as people acting on alternatives.

Systematic individuals will personalize only the alternative they intend to select. These people will weight all the alternatives before acting. While spontaneous individuals will try out an alternative to determine its worth, systematic individuals will gather information about a range of alternatives before trying out the idea. Its worth will be determined beforehand.

For systematic individuals, a decision to personalize or act on an alternative comes as the result of a complete analysis of the situation. Once an alternative is chosen, they will be reluctant to change that action because the decision is based on an analysis. Initial difficulties will be used as more data for analyzing the alternative's worth. If they have faith in their analytical skills, it will take a great deal of data to cause them to give up on a solution that they have previously determined to be correct. Thus in contrast to spontaneous individuals, systematic individuals will often be seen as persons thinking about alternatives.

It's not that the Spontaneous style is wishy-washy; it's just that a Spontaneous jumps around. They do what some call "personalizing" or "trying things on." Spontaneouses don't know how they feel about a decision until they do it. So for them, it's necessary to act in order to decide. The Spontaneous wants to try it on, see how it feels. Reactions like: "Hey, this feels great, I'm going to do this" or "Oh no, I don't like this, I'll have to try something else" guide them in deciding. This personalization process often creates problems but as Dennis the Menace succinctly told his dad:

"If I stopped to think before I did somethin', I wouldn't have time to do anything!"
--*Dennis the Menace,* February 16, 1984

The Systematic wants to decide and then act. The Spontaneous wants to try it on, see how it feels: 'Hey, this feels great, I'm going to do this.' to 'Oh, no, I don't like this, I'll have to try something else.' This is personalizing; it isn't a matter of right or wrong—though it certainly looks wrong to a Systematic. In a Doonsbury comic Mike, (the Systematic) cajoles Zonker (the Spontaneous) saying:

> "Maybe it is finally time to set yourself a serious goal in life. You can't just keep trying on lifestyles like so many party hats."
> --Doonesbury, November 16, 1986

Thinking Patterns

Another aspect of decision-making is the difference in the styles of thinking, which in turn may parallel in many ways a person's choosing behavior. The thought processes of the two styles are quite different. Spontaneous persons think in a thought-chaining manner that, when carried to its extreme, represents a stream-of-consciousness flow of ideas. They will often begin a conversation on one idea and end up talking about a completely different idea in a short time. When they need information for a decision or task, they can gather a large amount in a short period but will do so in this outwardly random or spontaneous manner.

　　The systematic is logical: "What are we going to do for our vacation?", my mother would ask my dad. My dad would go to AAA and get the trip sheet to see what the costs were. Once he had decided where we were going to go in a cost-effective way, my dad, the engineer, would analyze the trip. He would decide what would be the best route, where to stop, when to leave, etc., and all things considered, we would probably have a good time. (It was mandatory fun.)

Systematic individuals are logical in the thinking process. They move from thought to thought in a deliberate manner. They need time to gather information – information that is more detailed and analytical. They will approach this process in a logical or systematic manner.

A spontaneous doesn't work like that. He may look out and see a man in a blue-and-white shirt, and he might look at his tie, which matches his own tie, and that reminds him of the cover of a book he's reading. Then he remembers that the last time he was reading he was listening to his Walkman with the headphones, and the speaker fell out. He couldn't find the headphone since it fell in the grass. Then he begins to think of how much he hates cutting the grass, and that he had to do that when he got back from San Francisco, which is a really nice place to go, except it costs money. It's expensive in San Francisco.

That example is really easy for me to do because, as you're beginning to sense, that's my style. What I do is operate in a chaining kind of way, which links one idea to another to another to another. As soon as I start thinking about one idea, by the time I'm done, I'm all over the place. It's amusing to somebody who's a Systematic though they really think that Spontaneouses are kind of strange when they chain freely from one idea to another. I think the tension is epitomized in a quote given to me by a very Systematic partner:

> "**Spontaneous me,**" **sang (Walt) Whitman, and, in his innocence let loose the hordes of uninspired scribblers who would one day confuse spontaneity with genius.**"
> --Strunk & White, *Elements of Style*, p. 66

Of course, the stream-of-consciousness of the Spontaneous can have its drawbacks. I have a cartoon that shows ten birds with beaks to the sand, waves in the background and one commenting to another:

> "I forget what the hell we're looking for."

Such is a consequence of too rapid chaining.

One of my favorite cartoons is from Bob Thaves and takes place in Sid's Gourmet Diner where Sid declares to Frank and Ernest:

> "I don't have menus because I never know what it is going to be until it's cooked."
> --*Frank & Ernset*, June 26, 1987

As someone who likes to cook I completely understand. I never make something for company that I've made before — it takes the fun out of it knowing what might happen.

Risk Level

Another area that varies with decision-making style is the risk level and its consequences for action. When it comes to making decisions, once a situation is analyzed carefully, the Systematic is probably going to stay with the decision even if it doesn't seem to be working. Therefore, anytime the Systematic makes a decision, the consequences and the risks are perceived by them to be high. As a result Systematics are going to be a little slower when making a decision. Before they act, they need to think about the pluses and minuses.

Given the different approaches to goal orientation and evaluating alternatives, one senses that there would also be a difference in the speed with which individuals will commit to a new idea or goal. This is indeed the case, as Spontaneous individuals will typically move quickly to a new goal or to endorse a new idea.

Systematic individuals will not, however, move with the same speed as spontaneous individuals. They will be cautious in their choice of goals. Systematic individuals can decide quickly, but the decision is made in a qualitatively different manner from that of spontaneous individuals. In general, however, spontaneous individuals will decide on and commit to a new idea or goal much faster than systematic individuals. Let me elaborate.

For instance, if a Systematic decides he wants to be an accountant, and then attends some really horrible lectures, he could not easily change his mind. He may think, "This may be the wrong choice, but I've got to review my thinking. This job has money and security, so maybe it's just difficulty with the instruction. Maybe I need to study more. So I'll stay with the major, since it would probably be premature at this stage to bail out because I've been pretty careful about my analysis. Besides, I think my decision is probably right."

A spontaneous says, "Hey wait a minute. This isn't working." Everything happens quicker for the spontaneous. Everything has a lower risk level. The Spontaneous might say "Try something on and if it doesn't work, fine, try something else on."

So there are differences in styles that show up not only in terms of one's personal and professional life, but also in terms of what happens with smaller incidents. An extreme Systematic, won't even go to a restaurant, unless he's been there before. 'Well, I don't know if I want to go', he may say. Then when the Spontaneous does finally get a Systematic in the restaurant, the Systematic can't decide what to order. Usually something 'safe" is the choice, like chicken. The Spontaneous may say, 'Here's some octopus, there's some squid, we've never tried them before,' and the Systematic could reply, 'I might get sick; I'm not sure I'd like it'.

    Thus there are distinct differences in terms of the styles and levels of risk involved in making decisions for both the Systematic and the Spontaneous decision-makers in both low-stakes settings like the restaurant or in high stakes settings such as changing jobs.

    Remember, then…*Acting enables the Spontaneous to decide. Deciding enables the Systematic to act.*

Reaction To Events

As you might imagine, the two styles react quite differently to events. Ask a Systematic what he thinks of a movie. 'Well, the movie was different, and the cinematography was intersting. The creation of the heating and the plumbing systems was a nice parallel to the technology in our society. Parts of it were difficult to understand, and there was a slight hyperbole in there with the protagonists' mother.' But ask a Spontaneous: 'Wow, that was great! I loved it!' or 'This is the worst movie I have ever sat through!' They tend to either like or dislike something. They will not react to the component parts of the experience but to the totality.

For Spontaneous individuals, the first reaction to a question that asks for an analysis will be a holistic one. They can relate to the component parts of the experience but will usually not do so unless pressed to. In addition, spontaneous individuals have a tendency to over generalize feelings. If they have encountered a bad experience in one aspect of their lives, there will be a tendency to see all other parts of their lives as failing—for the Spontaneous it is as Yogi Berra once said, "I love movies if I like them."

Evaluations offered by Systematic individuals will generally be more tempered than that of spontaneous individuals. Systematic individuals will be less likely to pronounce an event as having extreme qualities (e.g., "great," "horrible"), as their analyses will find strengths and weaknesses in the event that would modify extreme assessments. The mood swings that may come for Spontaneous individuals in over generalizing an experience are probably less likely for Systematic individuals, who carefully categorize events.

TREASURE HUNTERS AND DETECTIVES

What I have found interesting is that, all other things being equal, the Spontaneous and the Systematic will come to make the same choice when faced with a similar problem. I first seriously wondered about this observation when I tested over 300 students in an introductory Chemistry class and found that only three-tenths of a point on the ACT Composite score separated the lowest performing group from the highest performing group. The largest difference on any of the subscales was 1.1 points. This similarity in decision-making raises some interesting questions: How could two such outwardly distinct styles lead to similar conclusions in decision-making situations? What is the nature of Systematic versus Spontaneous thought, i.e., is Spontaneous decision making a type of Systematic thought, or is it qualitatively different? To answer these questions I ended up exploring the literature of problem solving as it is now being applied in expert systems and think I've found an answer. (Expert systems are computer simulations of a subject matter expert's decision-making process)

Van Horn (1986) describes two of the most common search strategies in expert systems design as forward chaining and backward chaining.

- Forward chaining strategies begin with a small number of facts and use a series of decision rules to work toward the best answer. In forward chaining you start with the facts you can observe, draw conclusions about what they mean, ask questions and check things out, step by step, until you identify the problem and determine how to remedy it. (Van Horn, 1986, p. 111)

- Backward chaining strategies begin with a likely solution and work from that solution to find evidence that either confirms the solution or disproves it.

Van Horn illustrates the differences between backward and forward chaining by contrasting the strategies used by a treasure hunter working from an ambiguous map and those strategies used by a detective solving a murder:

- The seeker of hidden treasure uses forward reasoning. She starts with a set of clues and works forward step by step. At each stage she discovers new clues and narrows the number of possible locations. At last only one location remains.

- The detective, on the other hand, might use backward reasoning. He starts by considering a few of the most likely murder suspects and then works backwards to see which one best matches the available clues. "For it to be the butler, I would expect to find a motive, the means, and the lack of a good alibi. Do I find these?" (p.108)

On the next page is how Van Horn (p.110) summarized these strategies.

Attributes of Backward and Forward Chaining

Backward Chaining	Forward Chaining
Given a question, try to answer it.	Given a situation, try to respond to it.
Start by suggesting a possible solution to a problem, and then work backward to see if it is correct.	Start from the data given and work forward to a solution which is consistent with the data.
Test the hypothesis against the data available to see if the evidence supports it.	Examine the data available to find constraints which will limit the search.
Ask questions to seek data which will prove or disprove the hypothesis.	Apply the rules to generate plausible conclusions. Predict the best outcome, and compare the prediction to the data to find the best fit.

Here is how Van Horn (p.109) represented the processes visually:

Backward Chaining

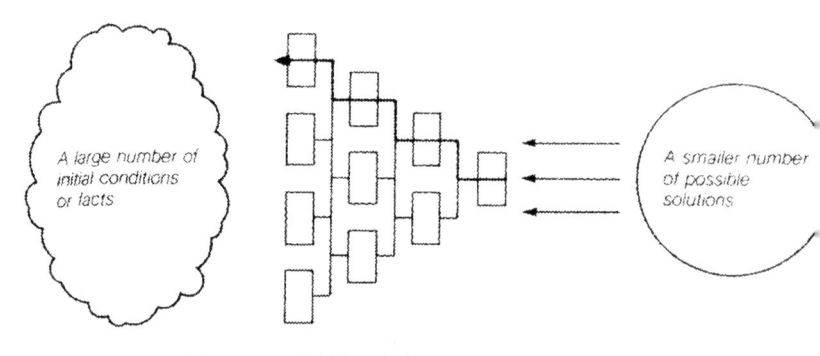

A large number of initial conditions or facts → [tree diagram] ← *A smaller number of possible solutions*

Forward Chaining

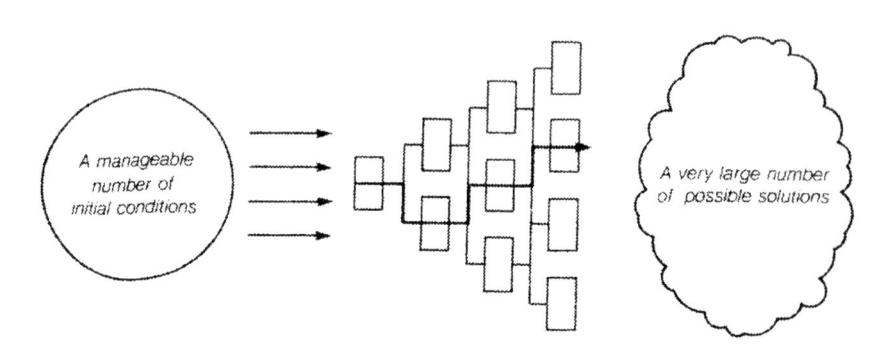

A manageable number of initial conditions → [tree diagram] → *A very large number of possible solutions*

In many ways I think that the information gathering styles are best understood as differences in reasoning — The Spontaneous Detective preferring a backward reasoning process and the Systematic Treasure Hunter a forward reasoning process.

Understanding Systematic and Spontaneous Information Gathering—An Example

In order to explore the differences between the Systematic and Spontaneous, it may be useful to create a simplified model of a decision-making situation. For purposes of illustration, consider the case of a college student choosing a career in a manner that best matches the individual's personal aptitudes and values with the characteristics of a selected career.

This illustration begins with six possible aptitudes or values the student will consider in selecting a career.

The aptitudes will be defined as:

- people skills or number skills.

The personal values will be defined as:

- high priority on income, low priority on income, high interest in travel, low interest in travel.

The possible career choices that could create a good match between aptitudes and values are:

- sales, counseling, geological engineering, or computer programming.

Here is a visual summary of this decision situation and shows it from top (careers in general) to bottom (career choices):

A career choice path

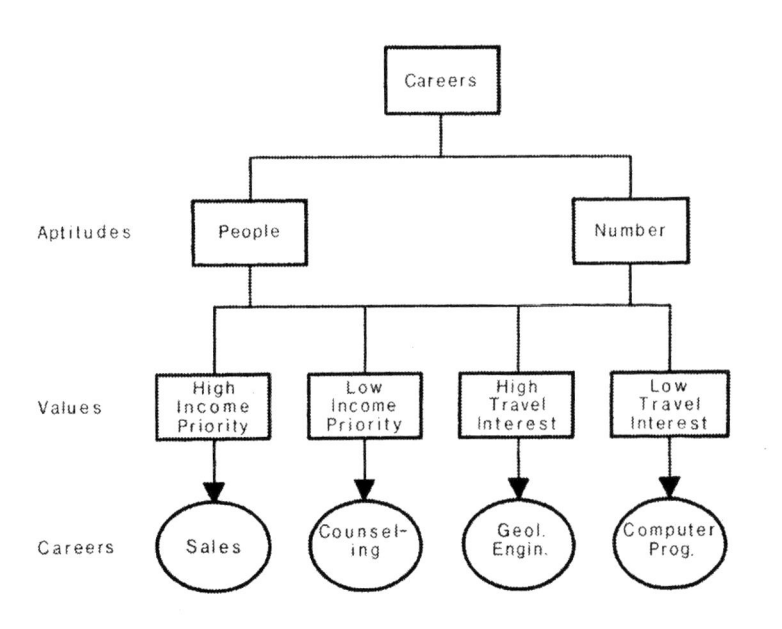

```
                         Careers
                        /        \
Aptitudes         People          Number
                  /    \          /     \
           High      Low      High      Low
Values    Income   Income    Travel    Travel
          Priority Priority  Interest  Interest
             |        |         |         |
Careers   (Sales) (Counsel- (Geol.   (Computer
                    ing)    Engin.)    Prog.)
```

Making the decision

The model case Systematic will probably begin the career selection process through a logical analysis of strengths, weaknesses, and interests. Data will be sought from friends, occupational libraries, and personality inventories. The data (cognitive and emotional) from these sources will be analyzed and weighed.

In this instance, the Systematic might recount the decision making process as follows:

> Well, it's hard to say exactly what led me to this career choice, but there were certain factors that seemed most important to me. First of all, I am a people oriented person. So much so, that I swear numbers will just fall out of my ears if I turn too fast. I couldn't balance a checkbook to save my life. So when I thought of my strengths and weaknesses, I just knew that any job I was going to be successful in had to avoid numbers.
> My next thought was that money is important to me. My family has a nice home and we have always been able to enjoy the things money brings. As I thought about it, it seems to me that a career in sales is one where there is no real limit to your income and one in which you deal with people, not numbers or machines.

Like the treasure hunter, the Systematic has used forward reasoning to solve a problem. This career choice was made by first identifying personal aptitudes, testing these aptitudes (as clues are tested), discarding the inappropriate alternative (number orientation), and then continuing this process to test, and select or discard other options as they apply to personal values (income). In the end, this path led to only one alternative (sales).

On the other hand, the model case Spontaneous will probably have declared a number of majors by the end of the first year of college. With each new declaration there is likely to be a strong and positive emotional commitment to the new career choice. After attending more classes, or perhaps imagining more thoroughly what it would be like to live with this career choice, the Spontaneous may abruptly announce a new occupational preference. The Spontaneous might recount this decision making process:

> I guess everyone thinks I'm a little crazy given the way I ended up in sales. Let's face it, I started by majoring in geological engineering, switched to counseling, majored in computer science and then ended up with sales--but I'm really comfortable with this choice and I think I'll be with it for quite a while.
>
> I know when I first began the engineering program sounded really interesting--geological engineering means lots of travel and I always wanted to do that. I had some problems with my physics classes though, and decided that maybe number things weren't really for me. I moved into counseling because I thought I might be able to get a job anywhere (and thus travel) and because I wanted out of my quantitative classes. By the end of that semester, I could see that this wouldn't work either--no income. I decided to

> give computers a try as programmers are in demand and I could probably move around as well. I really did think programming would be different than the math I didn't like, but I saw pretty quickly that they really do overlap.
> So by now I had about decided that numbers weren't for me, travel was nice, but that a good income was probably most important to living the way I'd like to live. As I thought about it, it struck me that a career in sales is one where there is no real limit to your income and one in which you deal with people, not numbers.

Like the detective, the Spontaneous uses backward reasoning to solve a problem. The career choice was made by first considering a few likely career choices that seem correct intuitively. As a commitment is made to a given career, new and unanticipated evidence about the career may arise. When some piece of evidence contradicts what was anticipated, a new choice is made. This process thus continues until the available evidence leads to a "correct" solution to the problem.

Unlike the Systematic who could identify their relevant aptitudes and values before decision-making, the Spontaneous is unable to talk about aptitudes and values until choices have been personalized. Further, these aptitudes and values become apparent only after a number of choices have been tried. While the Systematic is often able to articulate the components of a decision before the choice is made, the Spontaneous will have difficulty doing so. The articulation of the components of a decision is very difficult for the Spontaneous. These components form a unknown dimension to the Spontaneous that becomes known and explicit only through the hindsight that comes with personalizing the final choice.

In Conclusion

How could two such outwardly distinct styles as Spontaneous and Systematic thought lead to the similar conclusions in decision-making situations? It appears that:

- Systematic and Spontaneous thought are qualitatively different approaches to problem solving approaches best understood as Forward and Backward Reasoning processes, and

- Similar conclusions may be reached in similar situations by people of different styles due to a similar underlying cognitive structure or schema of the problem. This structure, hierarchical as was illustrated (or otherwise), is then processed using different search strategies, i.e., within the cognitive structure a Systematic may use a "top down" (Forward Chaining) approach to test alternatives, while the Spontaneous will work "bottom up" (Backward Chaining).

- All other things being equal, the same decisions may be made by people of different styles because they have each, in their own way, identified and tested all of the relevant decision points needed to make the decision. So it would seem that in some situations, as

Gladwell (2005, p.114) found after studying decision-making in a major war simulation and with a comedy improvization group "spontaneity isn't random."

Neither instance represents the one best way. Rather, if there is a one best way, it is probably best determined by the nature of the problem to be solved and the individual style of the decision maker. Treasure maps and murders call for different strategies; treasure hunters and detectives understand this, so should we.

PROCESSING STYLE: EXTERNAL & INTERNAL

There seems to be two processes by which information is analyzed—External and Internal. These focus not on how much people talk, but rather on the way in which they think. Individuals vary in the degree to which they are Internal or External processors as well as how talkative they are. In understanding these characteristics of internality and externality, one should always focus on what is being said rather than how much is being said.

External

The External person will need to think out loud. They will not be certain of a decision unless they have had the opportunity to talk about it. The more complex a decision, i.e., the more information that needs to be processed, the greater the need for discussion. It is not uncommon for external individuals to begin talking in favor of one opportunity and end up talking unfavorably of the same opportunity. This behavior should not be confused with the spontaneous characteristic of personalizing alternatives, but rather should be recognized as a need to hear their words to make sense of them. External individuals talk out loud to themselves when no one else is around to listen. These people think and talk simultaneously.

   Interestingly, Dennett (1991) in *Consciousness Explained*, argues that consciousness evolved as a way to internalize talking to oneself. Talking, externality, triggers parts of the brain involved in moving the diaphragm, tongue, lips, vocal chords, etc. Hearing words triggers parts of the brain connected to the ears. As one unkown author observed "Speaking aloud can be a bad survival strategy, especially when you're thinking about the chief's wife, so we developed consciousness as an internal monologue. It works, but it doesn't exercise as many areas of the brain as speaking and hearing your own words." (http://c2.com/cgi/wiki?RubberDucking, October 15, 2005)

This style, and for some *need*, to talk out loud as part of the thinking process has been termed, variously: "Rubber Ducking," "The Carboard Analyst," or "Teddy Bearing." Is summarized in *Creating Passionate Users* (2005). A story about this is in the book *The Practice of Programming* and goes something like this: a university help desk center kept a teddy bear, and before students were allowed to bring their problem to a human, they had to first explain it out loud to a teddy bear. The idea is that by the time they finished telling the bear, over half of them had solved their own problem. The technique is also known as rubberducking, because it doesn't matter much who or what you're talking to. It's the talking that matters. Explaining your problem out loud is often enough to shake things loose in your brain, expose bad assumptions, and cause you to see things in a new way."

Internal

Internal individuals prefer to do their processing privately before speaking. If pressed to discuss an issue they have not thought about, they will often become confused or irritated. Internal individuals need to introspect before making a decision. While External individuals need to think out loud, Internal individuals tell what they have already thought about. "Leave me alone, I want to think about that" is the mantra of the Internal. In a sense, the Internal acts like a submarine to efficiently and effectively achieve their goal — operating best when spared the surface currents of communication. But unlike the submarine that needs many people to function, the Internal wants to withdraw to be by themselves. They adapt a strategy I call "headphoning."

Headphoning is a technique I've come to use during travel. I just take out a pair of headphones, put them on, and put the plug in my pocket. I don't connect them to any source, but people around me assume I am listening to something and tend to respect my privacy.

THE FOUR BLENDED STYLES OF THE *DMSI*

Now I am going to blend the "primary colors" of the styles to create the four complete individual styles.

The Structural style defines how people gather information and has two ends on a continuum—Systematic and Spontaneous. The Structural style, by analogy, is like the wiring in an electronic circuit board—it's not bad or good it's just different. One kind of wiring gets you a television and another kind of wiring gets you a stereo.

The Processing style defines how people analyze information and has two ends on a continuum—Internal and External. By analogy, it is like the type of electricity that we use, alternating current vs. direct current. And again, there isn't a right or wrong to this dimension—it's just a difference. These four dimensions blend to create four styles.

The Detectives:
- Spontaneous-Internal,
- Spontaneous-External

The Treasure Hunters:
- Systematic-Internal
- Systematic-External

I do think that each of us has a preferred natural style, that we can use different styles at different times, but under stress we will tend to resort to that natural style.

On the next page is a swimming anlogy. If we think about how a swimmer needs to get from Point A on land to Point B on an island we can see how the styles might work.

Detectives and Treasure Hunters Go Swimming

The Systematic External will move from "A" to "B" in a way that you can always track—and is generally focused on a direct way to the goal.

The Systematic Internal will move toward B underwater. Their thoughts will be hidden. Like the swimmer they will surface for air, but will generally be found in the direction you expected them to be.

The Spontaneous External will jump in the water headed toward the goal—but can easily end up someplace totally different; but since they are External you will know where they are most of the time.

The Spontaneous Internal will dive into the water focused on the goal, but will chain onto new directions. They verbalize—surface—in directions you can't always predict by looking at the direction they last took.

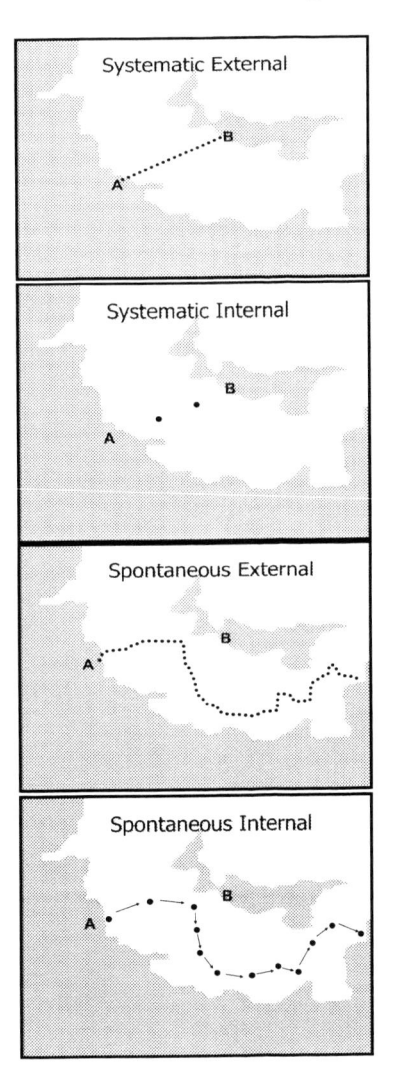

SUMMARY OF THE DMSI THEORY

The Spontaneous and Systematic dimensions are differentiated by five characteristics: goal orientation, choosing among alternatives, thinking patterns, speed of commitment to new ideas, and reaction to events.

The table on the next page summarizes these dimensions.

	Systematic	Spontaneous
Goal Orientation	• Moves from goal to goal in a deliberate manner. • Not likely to deviate from the goal.	• Moves from goal to goal easily and without deliberate thought. • A goal is easily forgotten or changed.
Choosing	• Weighs alternatives before acting. • A decision comes as the result of analysis. • Reluctant to change without strong reasons.	• Prefers action as a way to evaluate alternatives. • Needs to live with an idea, however briefly, to feel what it would be like. • Based on this feeling, they make a choice.
Thinking Patterns	• Logical in the thinking process. • Moves from thought to thought in a deliberate manner. • Wants time to gather detailed information.	• Thinks in a thought-chaining manner. • Thinking can chain based on thoughts, feelings, or outward stimuli. • Prefers to "jump in" rather than gather information.
Speed of a decision	• Cautious in their choice of goals. • Can decide quickly, but needs to reflect first..	• Not likely to worry about making a wrong decision. • Moves quickly to a new goal or idea.
Reaction to Events	• A reaction is detailed and focuses on the parts. • Evaluations offered are generally balanced.	• The reaction to an event is a "big picture." • Tends to either like or dislike something

The Internal and External dimensions are the two processes by which information is analyzed. These focus not on how much people talk, but rather on the way in which they think. Individuals vary in the degree to which they are internal or external processors as well as how talkative they are.

In understanding these characteristics of internality and externality, one should always focus on what is being said rather than how much is being said.

Internal	**External**
• Prefers to do their processing privately before speaking.	• Needs to think out loud.
• If pressed to discuss an issue they have not thought about, they will often become confused or irritated.	• Will not be certain of a decision unless they have had the opportunity to talk about it.
• Needs to introspect before making a decision.	• May talk out loud to themselves.
• Needs to think to talk.	• Needs to talk to think.

Here is one final way to think about the blended styles and their relationship to each other:

The DMSI Cube

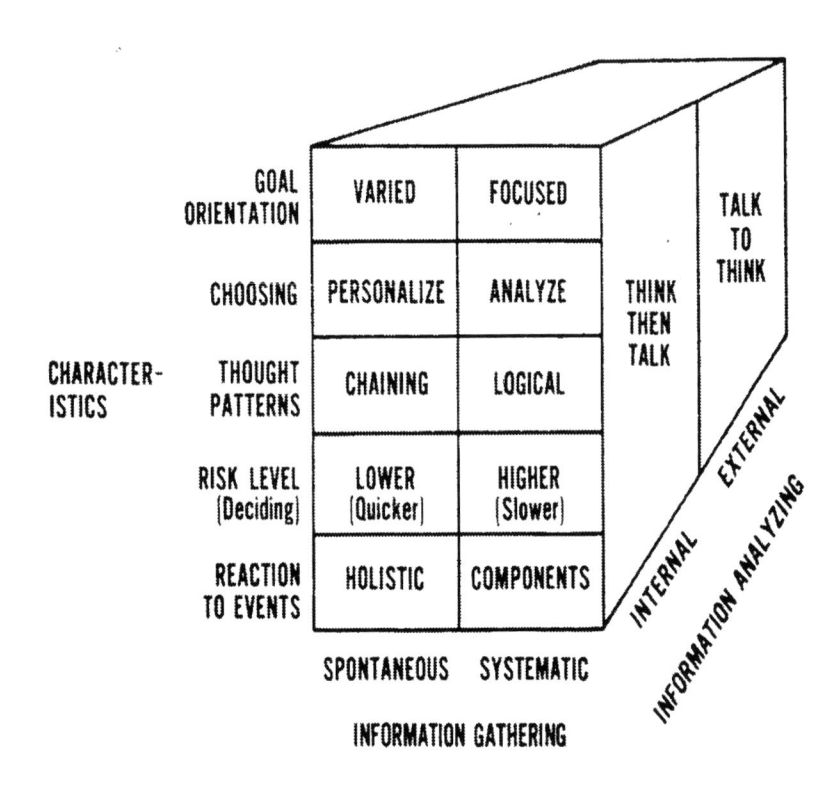

CHARACTER-ISTICS		VARIED	FOCUSED	THINK THEN TALK	TALK TO THINK
	GOAL ORIENTATION	VARIED	FOCUSED		
	CHOOSING	PERSONALIZE	ANALYZE		
	THOUGHT PATTERNS	CHAINING	LOGICAL		
	RISK LEVEL (Deciding)	LOWER (Quicker)	HIGHER (Slower)		
	REACTION TO EVENTS	HOLISTIC	COMPONENTS		
		SPONTANEOUS	SYSTEMATIC		
		INFORMATION GATHERING			

Axes: INTERNAL / EXTERNAL — INFORMATION ANALYZING

ASSESSING YOUR OWN STYLE [PART 2]

Earlier you made your a self-assessment of your *DMSI* style. Now that you have read more about the styles, look at the figure below.

1. What did you first choose as your style?

2. Would you change your assessment now? Why?

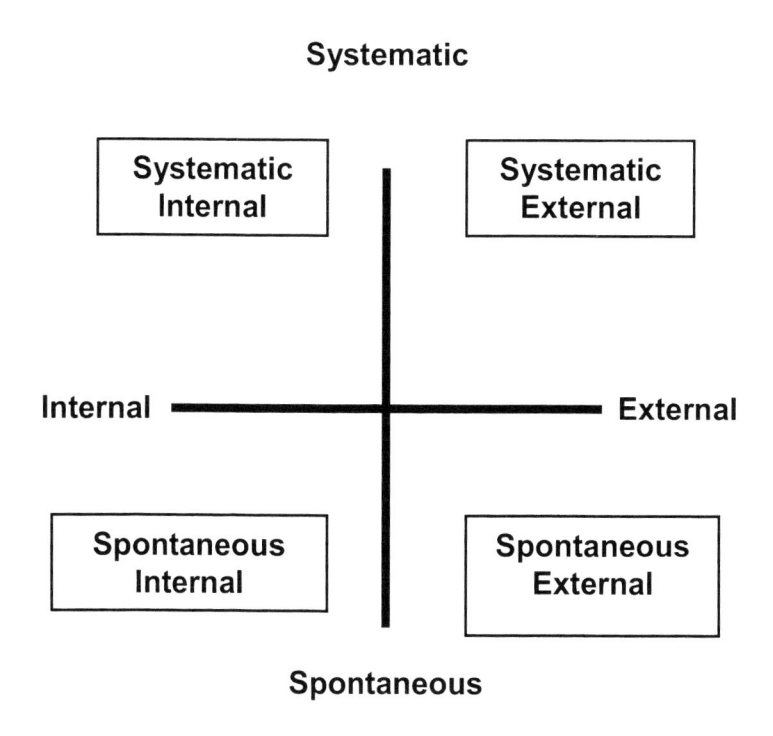

Systematic

Systematic Internal	Systematic External

Internal ——————————————— External

Spontaneous Internal	Spontaneous External

Spontaneous

THE STYLES IN ACTION

Although the *DMSI* theory was developed in a career counseling setting, it has proven useful in a variety of other environments. In alphabetical order, by topic, here are some qualities of the styles in action.

Art

One of my students (now anonymous) wrote an instructional unit on types of expository text. I was taken by how one of the passages the learners were asked to classify captured some of the essence of Spontaneous and Systematic action — and raising the issue of cultural differences in the style.

> **Our modern glass is exquisitely clear in its substance, true in its form, accurate in its cutting. We are proud of this. We ought to be ashamed of it.**
>
> **The old Venice glass was muddy, inaccurate in all its forms, and clumsily cut, if at all. And the old Venetian was justly proud of it.**
> **For there is this difference between the English and the Venetian workman, that the former thinks only of accurately matching his patterns, and getting his curves perfectly true and his edges perfectly sharp, and becomes a mere machine for rounding curves and sharpening edges, while the old Venetian cared not a whit whether his edges**

were sharp or not, but he invented a new design for every glass that he made, and never molded a handle or lip without a new fancy in it. And therefore, though some Venetian glass is ugly and clumsy enough, when made by clumsy and uninventive workmen, other Venetian glass is so lovely in its forms that no price is too great for it; and we never see the same form twice.

Now you cannot have the finish and the varied form too. If the workman is thinking about his edges, he cannot be thinking of his design; if of his design, he cannot think of his edges. Choose whether you will pay for the lovely form of the perfect finish, and choose at the same moment whether you will make the worker a man or a grindstone.

Career Counseling

In a freshmen orientation course at several universites these styles are used to help students grasp the nature of individual differences in career decision-making. For example, deciding on a career required different kinds of data for different styles. Systematic individuals seek a great deal of information (to be processed privately or in small groups – internal versus external) and choose cautiously. Spontaneous individuals want the "try on" majors, sometimes exploring as many as six before making a choice. The counselor realizes that each person has a preferred style of deciding and helps facilitate the process.

Film

The film literature also shows how creative minds come to bring their own styles unique outcomes. Alfred Hitchcock, for example, would not go to see his own movies. He had seen them in his mind so completely before the shooting he felt no further need to see the outcome. Charlie Chaplin was famous for spontaneously changing his movie as he shot it and in some instances ending up with a final movie that wasn't what he intended to do when he started.

In Umberto Eco's book *Travels in Hyperreality,* he talks of the making of the movie *Casablanca.*

> "Can I tell you a story?" Ilse asks. Then she adds: "I don't know the finish yet."
>
> Rick says: "Well, go on, tell it. Maybe one will come to you as you go along.
>
> Rick's line is a sort of epitome of Casablanca Eco writes. According to Ingrid Bergman, the film was apparently being made up at the time it was being shot. Until the last moment not even Michael Curtiz (the directior) knew whether Ilse would leave with Rick or with Victor, and Ingrid Bergman seems so fascinatingly mysterious because she did not know at which man she was to look with greater tenderness.

Interpersonal Relationships

One of the interesting differences between a Systematic and a Spontaneous is in terms of their personal relationships. For example, a Systematic looking at the end of a relationship may think, "Well, even if things aren't working out, we've got to give it a chance. I don't want to date a lot of different people. I may want this relationship, and I want to explore it in some depth. I want to be really certain if this relationship is right or wrong for me, and I want to be considerate of everybody concerned, in terms of whether to go on with the relationship or to end it."

The Spontaneous, in contrast may have dated eleven different people during the time the Systematic was exploring that one potential relationship. A Spontaneous may say, in effect, "Okay, let's date; let's have a good time. I don't want to necessarily deal with your style and who you are. If we don't agree, that's fine; let's try something else."

Friction often does occur between people of opposite types. For example, "She is always thinking about everything that happens in the relationship and just asks me why I did such and such (systematic internal), while I just want to do something different and talk about it" (spontaneous external) or "I can never really find out what is on her mind" (external-internal). Bringing these characteristics to light can begin a process of open communication between the parties. I used to think the Spontaneous-Systematic conflict would be the strongest one, but I've come to believe that it is actually the Internal-External clash that is most irksome with couples.

As it happens, I live with a very strong Internal. One Sunday morning I became increasingly concerned about the vision in one eye. I do wear glasses but things just didn't focus properly. As the morning progressed I became increasingly external about what was happening. By lunch I was planning a medical appointment for the next day.

All the while, this was happening with my Internal wife:

> What is that shiny spot by the sink? Oh my, it's a lens from William's glasses. I wonder what it's doing by the bathroom sink. He was probably in a hurry and just left it there for safekeeping until he has time to fix it. I'm sure he will fix it later.
> I think he went to wash the car. He did seem rather in a hurry to get outside. I wonder if he switched to another pair of glasses. Yes, I'm sure he did. Otherwise, everything would look crazy. I think his lens has popped out before. Was it the same pair of glasses? He really should get that thing fixed. He's probably distracted by the dizziness this morning. I wonder why he's dizzy. Strange for him. Oh well, back to the lens. Maybe I will mention it…
>
> [a couple of hours later]
>
> Oh, I see William's glasses lens is still there by the sink. I wonder why it's still there. He really should move it before it gets broken. Maybe I should move it to a safer place for him. It's going to get scratched. I could put it into an envelope for now. But really he should just go ahead and

>put it back into the frame. Maybe he tried already and couldn't fix it this time. I think he has extra glasses but those might be his favorites. How many pairs of glasses does he have anyway? And what about his dizziness? I better mention the lens...
>
>"William"…

And what of the External need to talk?

>The truth, the whole truth and nothing but the truth may do more harm than good to relationships, a University of Southern California study says.
>White lies, those seemingly harmless misconstructions of fact, actually may do more good for a relationship than a steady onslaught of honesty, said Dr. Kenneth Sereno, chairman of communications arts and sciences at the USC College of Letters, Arts and Sciences.
>"How can you be sensitive, thoughtful and caring if you just blurt out what's on your mind all the time?" Sereno said

As to managing these differences, my sense is that if you do it right, you get electricity; do it wrong and you'll have Chernobyl.

Personal Goals

I have edited here an interesting piece about externality that comes from Rabbi Noah Weinberg of Aish HaTorah. It is one of the most detailed discussions of the power of Externality I have read.

Way #3 Say It Out Loud

Articulate your beliefs out loud. It bridges the gap between lofty notions of the soul and the world of reality. In other words, you'll find out if you really believe what you say.

We come from a "quiet learning" society where "shhhh" is the rule. If you drop a book in a university library, people jump as if a bomb went off. Contrast this with a rabbinic study hall, where you're greeted by a rippling sea of sound. The uninitiated often ask: "How can these people learn with so much noise?!"

Arichat sfatayim literally means "arrange it on your lips." To gain more clarity and wisdom, try saying things out loud.

Sometimes you'll see a person walking down the street talking to himself. Do you recall ever doing this yourself? When? Why? It's a powerful concentration technique.

Articulate Your Principles for Life

Speech is a unique human characteristic. When

you want to translate something from a spiritual thought into a physical reality, speech is the method.

   When struggling with a question or problem, use your voice. It forces you to grapple with the strangeness and the vagueness. Bringing a thought from your mind into your mouth takes it from potential to actual. When we say it out loud, the thought becomes engraved in stone.
   Articulation bridges the gap between the demands of the body, and the lofty notions of the soul.
   This has practical application in synagogue life. During the silent "Amidah" prayer, people's lips are moving, though their voices are muted. And on Yom Kippur, the "Viduy" confession is said loud enough to hear yourself.
   Do you have difficulty talking out loud to yourself? Try writing instead. Keep a diary. Here's how to get started: Take a piece of paper and put it on the table in front of you. The paper calls for you to put something on it.
   The more senses you have working at one time, the deeper the impression. Saying something out loud means you are using every one of your bones. You are using your diaphragm, your brain, your ears, and your lips, teeth and tongue. Try to be consciously aware of involving every fibre of your being. When you

say "Hear O Israel, the Lord our God," do it from your toes. That makes a deep impression. It's living with everything you've got.

Why is "Saying It Out Loud" an Ingredient in Wisdom?

- Saying it out loud" helps you clarify fuzzy ideas.
- The more senses you involve, the more of an impression it leaves on you.
- What you speak is an expression of who you are.
- Everyone needs a sounding board, a feedback system. Do it yourself!
- Language is the bridge where body meets the soul.

Words are reality. "To say is to be!"

Sales

The world of sales is full of opportunities to use the styles. Being able to identify a customer's preferred style and working with them in their style will lead to a comfort zone that helps sales. Here are some thoughts on some basic steps in the sales process:

- Getting an appointment—Systematic Internals love notes in advance that are Systematic in nature. Spontaneouses are intrigued by novel stimuli. Something solid helps gets their attention. A three screen media production will have a stronger effect on the Spontaneous than on the Systematic. Externals may not be sure if they want to see you. Better get on the phone and talk to them about it--in either a Systematic or Spontaneous manner.

- Opening the call—Pace on the style. Pacing refers to matching a person with their own style. When I seek to create rapport with someone, one part of my strategy is to begin by identifying their preferred decision making style. I will then match or "pace" this style. This helps create comfort in the situation.

- Discovering buyer needs—In some situations, I may need to "lead" the buyer to another style that may be more appropriate for the task at hand. For example, if the contact is a Spontaneous, one needs to lead, or atl east plan, a Systematic approach to gathering all the data that might be relevant to the sale. An extreme Systematic may have to be led to more Spontaneous behavior in order to define all of the issues that are important in identifying a buyer's needs. In another instance, if one has identified that the contact is a Systematic--but that the decision-maker for the purchase is a Spontaneous supervisor--it will be important to understand that extended Systematic responses with the contact may prove useless in reaching the Spontaneous decision maker.

- Making the recommendation—Like the initial call, give the Systematic a lot of data in advance. Give the Externals time and attention in sorting out the recommendation. Keep the Spontaneous focused on the problem you have addressed.

- Asking for the business—he essence of decision-making style will develop here as this is the stage where the decision must be made. You will need to consider risk values, e.g., Spontaneouses are more likely to be risk takers than Systematics, etc.

- Installing and implementing—the Spontaneous is liable to forget about you and move onto a new problem. He or she will appreciate a follow-up call that touches on the most likely problems and solutions associated with your sale (that they have probably overlooked). The Systematic will appreciate a detailed analysis of the implementation plan. Externals will want to discuss things no matter how they are going.

Decision-making styles should be an important part of a sales repertoire. Remember, selling with style means knowing your style--and the styles of your client.

As an aside, I once made a presentation on using the styles for a Fortune 500 sales group. They *loved* it! By Friday afternoon I thought I had the sale. On Monday, it was on the back burner. I knew the people who were in the room Friday but I should also have known that if you have a room full of Spontaneouses it is best to sign the deal then and there rather than to wait [for them to chain on to something else!]

Task Groups

In task group settings, most groups fail to draw on individual styles for different aspects of the task. For example, spontaneous people are strongest in brainstorming, while systematic individuals excel in convergent activities such as evaluation of brainstorming suggestions.

    Groups also often fail to adjust for analysis styles. They usually proceed without giving internal individuals time to consider proposals or the external individuals time to meet and discuss a proposal. When was the last time you heard a group leader say, "OK, if the externals would move to another room to discuss the proposal and the Internals just stay here to think about it, we'll convene again in 20 minutes?

ADAPTATING YOUR STYLE

Individuals, regardless of their style, can adapt and use behaviors that tend to be associated with another style. For example, Spontaneous individuals can adapt to the requirements of some environments by setting goals and working at them in what seems to be a systematic fashion. Many times, however, such a person will still be using a style that is spontaneous. The goals may well be determined in a holistic manner, and the individual will move from one to the other with unnoticed flexibility.

Systematic individuals may adapt to a situation (e.g., a vacation) by "letting themselves go" and planning less. Although they seem spontaneous, many of the behaviors are structured and represent planned goals, for which the systematic individuals will adapt in a systematic manner. (Interestingly, it has been my experience that it is easier for a Spontaneous to shift to Systematic processes than the other way around.)

Internal individuals in a comfortable environment (i.e., probably low risk) can think and talk simultaneously. External individuals can ponder a problem for hours by themselves, but in neither case, will the results be as satisfactory as relying on one's dominant style.

It is sometimes difficult to identify a person's natural style when that person must adapt to a variety of settings. Adults may often have a style that works best for their professional life but is different than from their personal life.

The theory's most obvious strength lies in its ability to make clarify and manage many of our felt understandings of individual differences.

WHY THESE FOUR STYLES?

We know how these styles came to be recognized—from listening to hundreds of people talk about choices in their lives. But there is a final question here that isn't likely to be answered in the near future: "Why these four styles?" The only answer now is another question: "Who knows?" The issue of individual differences in personality has piqued the curiosity of people through thousands of years since the Egyptians tried to find meaning to human behavior though the Zodiac.) But as one researcher observed "No one has ever seen personality." (Murphy-Paul, 2004, p. 199) Murphy-Paul also goes on to summarize some of the current research in personality noting:

> the increased interest in biological causes of personality. We know, for example, that Introverts use different parts of their brain than Extroverts. Canli believes that discrepancies in the brain scans reveal "intrinsic differences in the way people with varied personalities process information about the world. Extroverts (based on a short form of the NEO PI-R), it seems, are wired to respond automatically and affirmatively to positive stimuli, while introverts are not. Such individual differences in brain reactivity, he says amount to a person's 'neural signature.' (in Murphy-Paul, p. 200)…in the meantime, other biological approaches are yielding additional insights into personality. For example, research indicates that that the nervous systems of introverts are more sensitive than those of extroverts making them more likely to startle at a loud sound…Analyses of the electroconductivity of the skin demonstrate that anxious and neurotic individuals settle down less quickly after they've been stressed…Assays of

various chemicals swimming in our bloodstreams offer another source of information...and DNA analysis has begun to connect specific genes to particular personality traits...individuals who inherit one form of (dopamine receptors) tend to be excitable and impulsive; they may be diagnosed with higher rates of attention deficit disorder, and they may be more likely to abuse drugs. (pp. 200-202)

More evidence continues to emerge about the physiological underpinnings of choice. Damasio (in Gladwell, 2005) studied patients with damage to a part of the brain associated with decision-making—the ventromedial prefrontal cortex. He describes trying to set up an appointment with a patient who had this damage:

> I suggested two alternative dates, both in the coming month and just a few days apart from each other. The patient pulled out his appointment book and began consulting the calendar. The behavior that ensued...was remarkable. For the better part of the half hour, the patient enumerated reasons for and against each of the two dates: previous engagements, proximity to other engagements, possible meteorological conditions, virtually anything that one could think about concerning a simple date. [He was] walking us through a tiresome cost-benefit analysis, an endless outlining and fruitless comparison of options and possible consequences. It took enormous discipline to listen to all this without pounding on the table and telling him to stop. (pp. 59-60)

This so closely mirrors the situation of the "agonizing decision maker" that one must consider that there are biological roots to many of our differences in processing.

John Cecil, (personal communication, October 27, 2005) a physician working with Attention Deficit Hyperactive Disorders for more than 20 years, likened the distinction between Spontaneous and Systematic styles to brain development starting with pre-historic humans. The Hunter-Gatherer distinction reflects to some degree the organization of the brain into two classes: The Hunter (Spontanoeus) who needed to constantly scan the environment for purposes of security and food; the Gatherer (Systematic) who needed to carefully understand the soil for growing, the local resources, the nature of the seasons, etc. and as a result they developed different operations in the pre-frontal cortex that can be seen in MRIs. (2005, personal communication)

Tourette's Syndrome can have as part of its range of symptoms uncontrollable vocal utterances. Some point to chemical transmission with dopamine and/or serotonin and their respective receptor sites research (Society for Neuroscience, 1998). Perhaps Externality is also a chemical issue.

My studies have shown a pattern of styles in USA samples: 45% tend to be Systematic-Internals, 35% Systematic-Externals, 11% for Spontaneous-Externals, and 9% for Spontaneous-Internals. However, even if the percentages vary, the order tends to be the same. The theory was developed in an inductive way by listening to hundreds of college students without regard to an a priori theoretical approach.

So for whatever reason, then, the styles do seem exist—but as to why, who knows?

REFERENCES

1. Cartalk. (2002). Age activated attention deficit disorder: This is how it goes. cartalk.cars.com/Mail/Haus/2002/06.15.htm

2. Chabon, M. (1988). *The Mysteries of Pittsburgh.* New York: Harper-Collins.

3. Coscarelli, W. C. (1983). Decision making styles in the group process. *Performance and Instruction,* **22**(7), 22-25.

4. Coscarelli, W. C. (1983). Development of a decision-making inventory to assess Johnson's decision-making styles. *Measurement and Evaluation in Guidance,* **16**, (3), 149-160.

5. Coscarelli, W. C. (1987). Selling: Differences in deciding. *Sound Management,* **4**(8), 26-27.

6. Coscarelli, W. C. (1983). Decision making styles in the group process. *Performance and Instruction,* 22(7), 22-25.

7. Coscarelli, W. C., & Stonewater, J. (1984). Psychological typologies and the dynamics of consultant relationships. In R. Bass & C. Dills (Eds.), *Instructional development: The state of the art, II* (pp. 275-288). Dubuque, IA: Kendall/Hunt.

8. Coscarelli, W. C., & Stonewater, J. K. (1979-80). Understanding psychological styles in instructional development consultation. *Journal of Instructional Development Consultation,* **3**(2), 16-18, 21-22.

9. Coscarelli, W. C., Stepp, S. L., & Lyerla, R. (1989). Relationship of Blood Type with Decision-Making Style and Personality Type. *The Mankind Quarterly*, 29(4), 1989.

10. Coscarelli, W., Burk, J. and Cotter, A. (1995). HRD and decision-making styles. *Human Resources Development Quarterly*. **6**(4), 383-395.

11. Creating Passionate Users. (October 12, 2005) *Rubber Ducking and Creativity*. http://headrush.typepad.com/creating_passionate_users/2005/01/rubberducking_a.html

12. Cross, D. (1983). *Mediaspeak: How television makes up your mind*. New York: Coward McCann.

13. Dennett, D. (1991). *Consciousness Explained*. Boston: Little, Brown, & Company.

14. Di Vinci, Leonardo. (1506-1510). *Codex Leicester*. 2B Left panel.

15. Gladwell, M. (2005). *Blink: the power of thinking without thinking*. New York: Little, Brown, and Company.

16. Green, R. (1983). *American Beat*. New York, Atheneum.

17. Gordon, V. N., Coscarelli, W. C., & Sears, S. J. (1986). Comparative assessments of individual differences in learning and career decisions. *Journal of College Student Personnel*, **27**(3), 233-242.

18. Heischmidt, K. and Coscarelli, W. (1995). Consumer attitudes important in choosing lawyers and accountants according to decision-making style. *Journal of Professional Services Marketing*, 12(2), 49-67.

19. *Indianapolis Star* (1982). November, 25, p. 53.

20. Johnson, R. H. (1978). Individual styles of decision-making: A theoretical model for counseling. *Personnel and Guidance Journal*, 27, 530-536.

21. King, S. (1997). Speech on C-SPAN, January 1.

22. Miller, D. (1991, January). What Jefferson and Lincoln read. *Atlantic Monthly*, p.56.

23. *Newsweek* (1979). Books. August 20, p. 69.

24. Paul, A.M. (2004). *The cult of personality: How personality tests are leading us to miseducation our children, mismanage our companies, and misunderstand ourselves.* New York: Free Press.

25. Riggs, D. (2005) News Q3/05. *BMW Magazine*, p.12)

26. Serano, K. (1986). In Webster, B. Want to stay married? Forget the total honesty, study shows. *St. Louis Post Dispatch*, November 30, p. 13D.

27. *Society for Neuroscience* (1998) (http://apu.sfn.org/content/Publications/BrainBriefings/tourettes.html) (September 27, 2005)

28. Strain, B. & Wysong, P. (1979) *Communication skills*. Reading, MA: Addison-Wesley.

29. Tallman, I., & Gray, L. (1990). Choices, decisions, and problem-solving. *Annual Review of Sociology*, 16, 405-433.

30. Van Horn, M. (1986). *Understanding expert systems*. New York: Bantam Books.

31. Weinberg, N. (October, 2005) http://www.aish.com/spirituality/48ways/Way_3_Say_It_Out_Loud.asp